MOOSE RACKS, BEAR TRACKS,
AND OTHER
ALASKA KIDSNACKS

Cooking with kids has never been so easy!

Written by Alice Bugni
Illustrated by Shannon Cartwright

PAWS IV
PUBLISHED BY SASQUATCH BOOKS

P9-BYE-818

Printed in China

09 08   9 8 7

Library of Congress Cataloging in Publication Data
Bugni, Alice.
      Moose racks, bear tracks, and other Alaska kidsnacks : cooking with kids has never been so easy /
written by Alice Bugni : illustrated by Shannon Cartwright.
      p. cm.
      Summary: A recipe book featuring fun foods with Alaska-based names, such as Bear tracks, Denali
peaks, and Kayaks.
      ISBN 1-57061-214-5
      1. Cookery Juvenile literature. [1. Cookery.] I. Cartwright, Shannon, ill. II. Title.
      TX652.5.B747 1999
      641.5' 123—dc21

                                                      99-14003

PAWS IV
Published by Sasquatch Books
119 South Main Street, Suite 400
Seattle, Washington 98104
(206) 467-4300
www.SasquatchBooks.com
Custserv@SasquatchBooks.com

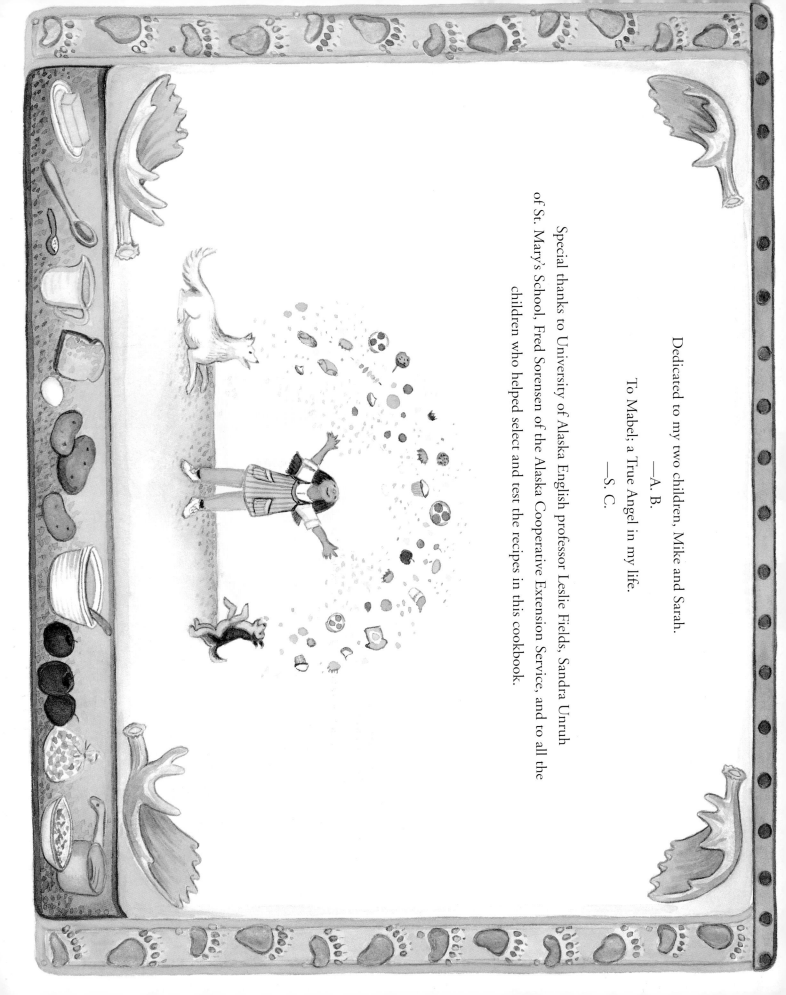

Dedicated to my two children, Mike and Sarah.

—A. B.

To Mabel; a True Angel in my life.

—S. C.

Special thanks to University of Alaska English professor Leslie Fields, Sandra Unruh of St. Mary's School, Fred Sorensen of the Alaska Cooperative Extension Service, and to all the children who helped select and test the recipes in this cookbook.

About the Author and the Illustrator

Alice Bugni was born in Juneau, Alaska, and raised in Seattle, Washington. She returned to Alaska in 1974 to work on the trans-Alaska pipeline and married a Kodiak fisherman. Alice has lived in Kodiak ever since, raising two children and finding creative ways to get through the long, dark winters. *Moose Racks, Bear Tracks, and Other Alaska KidSnacks* began as a winter project collecting favorite snack recipes for kids. Alice's current hobby is genealogy—tracing her ancestry back to the Tlingits of Southeast Alaska.

Pipi Bugni Leonard

For more than twenty years, **Shannon Cartwright** has been creating the illustrations for the best-selling PAWS IV children's books. A native of Michigan, she says, "Finding Alaska was the best thing that ever happened to me. This is my home." Shannon and her husband live in the Talkeetna Mountains, 25 miles from the nearest road. When not illustrating books, Shannon spends her time making jewelry or traveling through the mountains with her ponies and her dog, Cirrus.

Introduction

Cooking with my five-year-old daughter was always a lesson in patience. It seemed that every time we looked away from the cookbook, our recipe disappeared. So I devised a method that made it easier for her—I printed the recipe onto one page, in large print, and taped it onto the cupboard where we both could see it.

When I taught a second-grade cooking class, I learned that just being able to read the recipe wasn't enough—the kids had to like what they were making or they quickly lost interest. So, I began collecting recipes that kids would like to cook. The result is *Moose Racks, Bear Tracks, and Other Alaska KidSnacks*—an Alaska-theme cookbook with fun, easy-to-make, snack-food recipes, each with a title and lively illustrations inspired by the people, land, and animals of the Great Land.

Most of the recipes require minimal parental guidance, making them ideal for adults and their kitchen helpers ages five and up. Some, however, involve the use of a hot stove, heated oil, hot grease, or a sharp knife, and require extra guidance and caution. The simple ingredients and clear instructions guarantee quick results and yummy success. So cook up some of these recipes with your kids and watch them beam with pleasure at the tasty results. Best of all, they'll feel as though they created their "Alaska kidsnack" all on their own!

CONTENTS

MIDNIGHT SUN breakfast toast with fried egg center

MOOSE RACKS chewy and sweet caramelized bacon strips

MUSKOX MORSELS coated cereal squares that melt in your mouth

OCTOPUS'S GARDEN gelatin cups with fruit and whipped topping

PORCUPINES sticky rice cereal balls

PUFFINS candy-coated popcorn

SEA OTTER BISCUITS double chocolate chip cookies from a cake mix

SNAILS rolled and baked pie crust wedges

THREE BEARS' BREAD chocolate gingerbread muffins

TOTEM POLES fresh fruit kebabs

TUNDRA TURF an apple crisp with a homemade crust

WILDERNESS TRAIL MIX teriyaki-flavored cereal squares

WOLVERINES peanut butter balls coated in chocolate

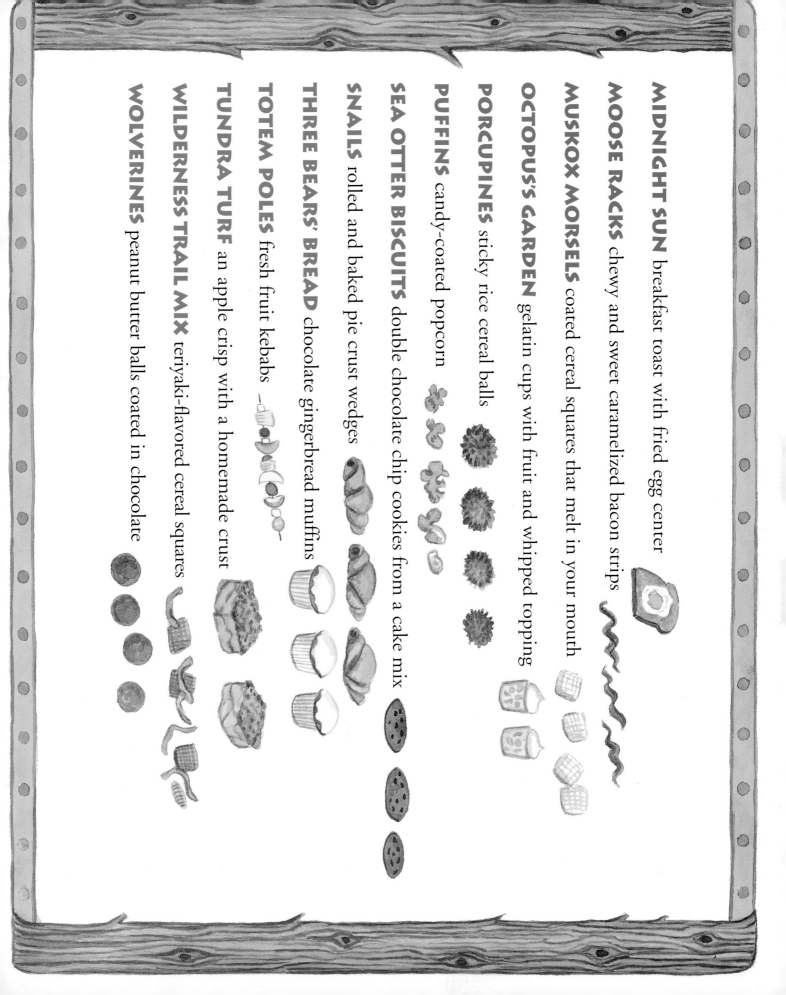

ARCTIC ANIMAL CRACKERS

2 cups flour
1 teaspoon salt
2 teaspoons baking powder
½ cup unsalted butter
1 cup sugar
1 egg
1 teaspoon vanilla
¼ cup milk

In a medium bowl, combine flour, salt, and baking powder; set aside. Using a mixer, cream butter and sugar in a large bowl; beat in egg, vanilla, and milk. Add flour mixture, cover, and chill 1 hour. Preheat oven to 375°. Lightly grease a cookie sheet. Roll dough ¼-inch thick on floured board and cut with cookie cutters. Bake on cookie sheet for 8 to 10 minutes. Makes about 2 dozen.

Polar bear, walrus, and caribou roam the great white arctic they call home.

BEAR TRACKS

¾ cup peanut butter
¼ cup brown sugar
1 teaspoon vanilla
1 can (14 ounces) sweetened condensed milk
2 cups all-purpose baking mix
1 package (4 ounces) slivered almonds

Preheat oven to 350°. In a large bowl, combine peanut butter, brown sugar, vanilla, and condensed milk. Stir in baking mix. Shape dough into 1½-inch balls, and insert 5 almond slivers on the side of each cookie. Place on ungreased cookie sheet and bake for 8 to 10 minutes. Makes about 2 dozen.

Bustling bears leave footprint trails near salmon streams and blueberry hills.

BEAVER DAM

6 cups honey graham cereal squares
2 cups chocolate chips
1½ cups mini-marshmallows

Preheat oven to 450º. Spread cereal squares onto foil-lined cookie sheet. Distribute chocolate chips and marshmallows evenly over cereal squares. Bake for 2 minutes and remove from oven. Lift edges of foil toward center of pan, blending ingredients together. Makes 7 cups.

Using branches, mud, and stones,
the beavers build their dams and homes.

BIG DIPPERS

6 small apples
6 popsicle sticks
1 package (14 ounces) caramels, unwrapped
1 cup mini-marshmallows
1 tablespoon water
1 cup crushed cereal or chopped nuts

Lightly grease a foil-lined cookie sheet. Rinse apples and insert popsicle stick into stem end. In a medium saucepan, heat caramels, marshmallows, and water over medium-low heat, stirring until creamy and smooth. Remove from heat. Dip apples into caramel. Dip bottom end into crushed cereal or nuts. Place on prepared cookie sheet. Refrigerate 20 minutes to harden. Makes 6.

*Alaska's flag proudly waves
a shiny golden star display.*

DENALI PEAKS

3 tablespoons butter, room temperature
3 tablespoons brown sugar
⅔ cup milk
2⅓ cups all-purpose baking mix

Glaze:

¾ cup sifted powdered sugar
1 tablespoon hot milk or water

Preheat oven to 450º. Lightly grease a cookie sheet. Using a mixer, cream butter and sugar in a large bowl; add milk. Stir in baking mix. Drop by spoonfuls onto cookie sheet. Bake for 10 to 12 minutes. Cool. Stir together glaze ingredients and drizzle over scones. Makes 1 dozen.

Known to many as Mount McKinley— our highest peak, the great Denali.

EAGLE'S NEST

3 cups stick pretzels
1 cup dry-roasted peanuts
1 cup raisins
1 cup mini-marshmallows
2 cups chocolate chips
2 teaspoons oil

Combine pretzels, nuts, raisins, and marshmallows in a large bowl; set aside. In a small saucepan, heat chocolate chips and oil over low heat, stirring constantly until chips melt. Pour chocolate over pretzel mixture, stirring until all pieces are evenly coated. Spoon into muffin tins and refrigerate 20 minutes to harden. Makes about 2 dozen.

An eagle's nest perched high above is built to last with sticks and mud.

GLACIER ICE

1 package (16 ounces) frozen strawberries, undrained
1 tablespoon lemon juice

Combine frozen strawberries and lemon juice in a food processor; whirl just until blended. Pour chunky mixture into a reclosable plastic freezer bag and freeze 3 hours. Remove from freezer, spoon into food processor, and whirl until almost smooth; do not over process. Return to freezer for 3 to 4 more hours. Remove sorbet from freezer 15 minutes before serving. Makes 2 cups.

Flowing down the mountainside,
ancient rivers of ice collide.

HIGHLINER PIES

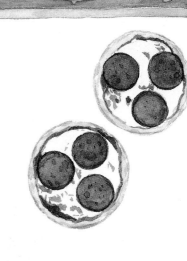

1 box (2 pounds) pilot bread crackers
1 jar (14 ounces) pizza sauce
1 bag (12 ounces) shredded mozzarella cheese
1 package (3.5 ounces) sliced pepperoni

Preheat oven to 425°. Line a cookie sheet with foil. Spread 1 tablespoon pizza sauce onto each cracker. Sprinkle with cheese. Place 3 pepperoni slices on top, place on cookie sheet, and bake for 3 to 4 minutes. Makes 18.

The first fishermen to catch the most are fishing on a Highliner boat.

IDITAROD TRAIL MIX

1 teaspoon cinnamon

½ teaspoon each allspice, nutmeg, ginger, and salt

½ cup brown sugar

1 egg white

2 tablespoons cold water

4 cups pecans, walnuts, almonds, or other nuts

Preheat oven to 275°. Lightly grease a foil-lined cookie sheet. Combine spices, salt, sugar, egg white, and water in a large bowl and whisk until blended. Add nuts, stirring until evenly coated. Drain coated nuts in a colander. Place on cookie sheet and bake for 35 minutes. Cool, then break apart. Makes 4 cups.

Excited huskies hurry ahead to cross the finish line with their sled.

KAYAKS

2 large baking potatoes, scrubbed
2 tablespoons vegetable oil
2 teaspoons onion salt

Preheat oven to 450°. Lightly grease a foil-lined baking sheet. Cut potatoes lengthwise into 8 wedges. In a large bowl, toss potatoes with oil. Sprinkle with onion salt. Place wedges in single layer on baking sheet. Bake for 25 to 30 minutes, or until potatoes are golden brown and tender when pierced with a fork. Makes 16.

A vessel of seal skin or caribou hide carries one hunter seated inside.

LAST FRONTIER CEREAL

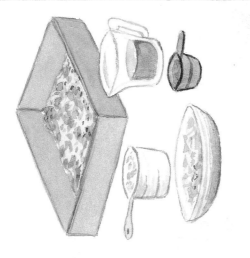

½ cup honey
⅓ cup vegetable oil
3 cups rolled oats
½ cup dry milk, sifted
½ cup sesame seeds
1½ cups coconut
1 cup sunflower seeds
1 cup wheat germ
1 cup slivered almonds

Preheat oven to 300°. In a small saucepan, heat honey and oil until warm; set aside. In an 11- by 14-inch baking pan, combine remaining ingredients; pour honey mixture over all, stirring until evenly coated. Bake for 45 minutes, stirring every 15 minutes. Remove from oven. As mixture cools, stir to break apart. Makes 8 cups.

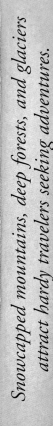

Snowcapped mountains, deep forests, and glaciers attract hardy travelers seeking adventures.

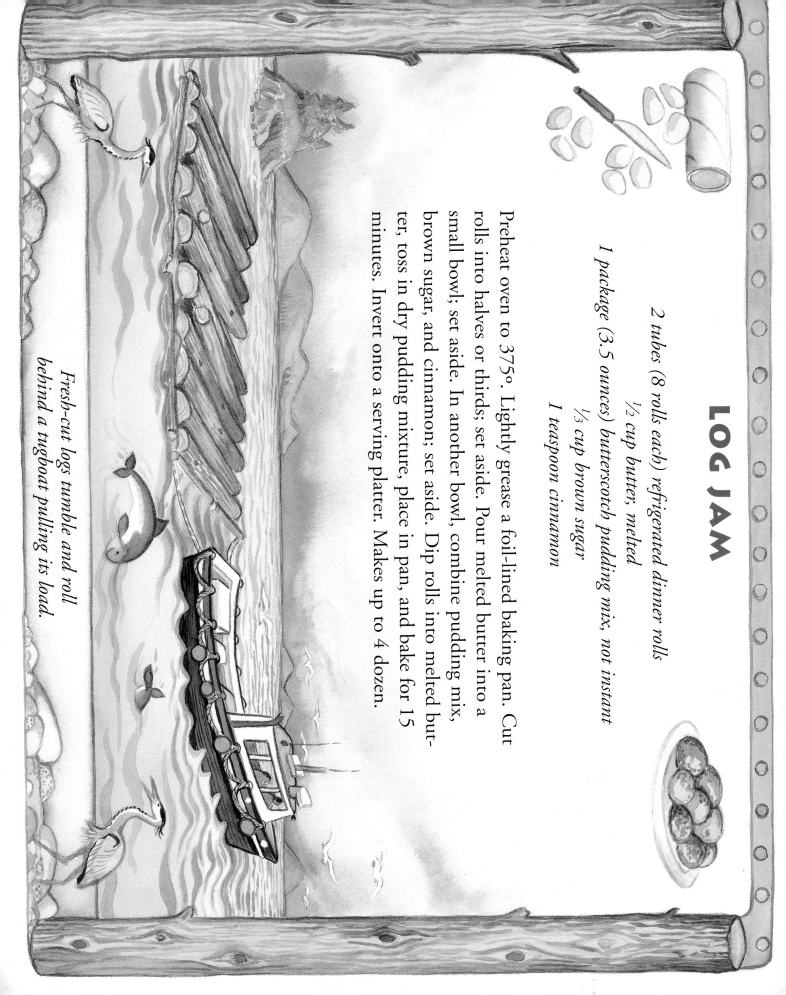

LOG JAM

2 tubes (8 rolls each) refrigerated dinner rolls

½ cup butter, melted

1 package (3.5 ounces) butterscotch pudding mix, not instant

⅓ cup brown sugar

1 teaspoon cinnamon

Preheat oven to 375°. Lightly grease a foil-lined baking pan. Cut rolls into halves or thirds; set aside. Pour melted butter into a small bowl; set aside. In another bowl, combine pudding mix, brown sugar, and cinnamon; set aside. Dip rolls into melted butter, toss in dry pudding mixture, place in pan, and bake for 15 minutes. Invert onto a serving platter. Makes up to 4 dozen.

Fresh-cut logs tumble and roll behind a tugboat pulling its load.

MIDNIGHT SUN

1 slice bread
1 tablespoon butter
1 egg
Salt and pepper

Use a glass to cut out the center of the slice of bread. Butter both sides of bread. Place buttered bread in a hot frying pan. Brown slightly, then break the egg into the hole in the center. When bread is browned, turn over gently and cook the other side. Sprinkle with salt and pepper. Makes 1.

Endless hours of midnight sun
make Alaskan summers a lot more fun!

MOOSE RACKS

1 pound thinly sliced bacon
1 tablespoon sesame seeds
1 cup brown sugar

Preheat oven to 375°. Line an 11- by 14-inch baking pan with foil. Cut bacon strips in half and arrange in prepared pan in a single layer. Bake for 10 minutes, then turn and sprinkle with sesame seeds and brown sugar. Return to oven and bake another 10 minutes. Remove to a slightly greased platter to cool. Makes about 36 slices.

A bull's spiked and spoon-shaped antlers fall off during cold mid-winter weather.

MUSKOX MORSELS

1 cup peanut butter chips
½ cup smooth peanut butter
⅓ cup butter
8 cups rice cereal squares
1 cup powdered sugar, sifted

In a large pot, melt chips, peanut butter, and butter over medium-low heat, stirring constantly until creamy and smooth. Remove from heat, add cereal, and stir until all pieces are evenly coated. Pour powdered sugar into a large paper bag, add cereal mixture, and shake until all pieces are evenly coated. Dry on a foil-lined cookie sheet. Makes 8 cups.

Long-haired, woolly, shaggy, and stout,
the muskox nibbles with his big, soft snout.

OCTOPUS'S GARDEN

1 can (15 ounces) fruit cocktail, drained
10 plastic drinking cups, about 9 ounces
1 package blueberry- or lime-flavored gelatin
1 container whipped topping

Divide fruit cocktail equally among cups; set aside. Prepare gelatin according to package directions and pour into fruit cups. Chill 3 hours, or until set. Serve topped with whipped topping. Makes 10.

Gliding out of its rocky den, the eight-tentacled octopus goes hunting again.

PORCUPINES

5 cups cocoa rice cereal
¼ cup butter
4 cups mini-marshmallows

Pour cereal into a large bowl; set aside. In a large pot, melt butter and marshmallows over low heat, stirring until mixture is creamy and smooth. Remove from heat, add cereal, and stir until evenly coated. Let mixture cool 5 minutes, then with greased hands, work quickly to shape mixture into 2-inch balls. Makes 8.

Up and down valleys the porcupine searches for savory bark and tasty deer antlers.

PUFFINS

20 cups popped popcorn
1 package (20 ounces) vanilla-flavored candy coating
3 tablespoons peanut butter

Place popcorn in a large bowl or other container. Line a table top with waxed paper. In a medium saucepan, melt candy coating and peanut butter on low heat, stirring until creamy and smooth. Pour over popcorn and stir until evenly coated. Spread mixture onto waxed-paper-lined table top, in a single layer, and let dry for 20 minutes. Makes 5 quarts.

Plump clown parrots, with bright-orange feet,
Live where the ocean and rocky cliffs meet.

VANILLA COATING

SEA OTTER BISCUITS

1 box chocolate cake mix
½ cup oil
2 eggs
1 cup chocolate chips

Preheat oven to 375º. In a large bowl, combine cake mix, oil, and eggs, stirring until blended. Stir in chocolate chips. Drop by teaspoonfuls onto ungreased cookie sheets. Bake for 8 to 10 minutes. Cool completely before removing from cookie sheet. Makes 3 dozen.

Furry, sleek, and content to float, otters munch urchins and groom their coats.

SNAILS

¼ *cup sugar*
½ *teaspoon cinnamon*
1 *box (2-crust size) "unfold and bake" refrigerated pie crusts*
¼ *cup butter, melted*

Preheat oven to 350º. In a small bowl, mix sugar and cinnamon; set aside. Unfold crusts and brush with some of the butter, sprinkle with some of the sugar mix, and cut like a pie into 8 wedges each. To make snails, roll each slice from the outer edge toward the tip. Place on ungreased baking sheets, brush with butter, and sprinkle with sugar mix. Bake for 12 to 15 minutes. Makes 16.

Inching along the ocean floor,
snails carry their home wherever they go.

THREE BEARS' BREAD

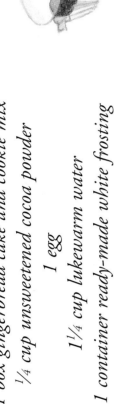

1 box gingerbread cake and cookie mix
¼ cup unsweetened cocoa powder
1 egg
1¼ cup lukewarm water
1 container ready-made white frosting

Preheat oven to 350º. In a large bowl, combine gingerbread mix, cocoa powder, egg, and water. Stir until well blended. Fill muffin cups half full and bake for 17 to 20 minutes. Top with white frosting. Makes 1 dozen.

Bears eat all summer until they are fat, preparing to take their long winter's nap.

TOTEM POLES

Fresh fruit of your choice
Maraschino cherries
Canned pineapple chunks
Mini-marshmallows
Kebab skewers

Cut fresh fruit into sections. Drain cherries and pineapple chunks. Arrange fresh fruit, cherries, pineapple chunks, and marshmallows on skewers in a colorful and appealing manner. Serve immediately.

Carved from cedar; these poles tell tales of Raven, Eagle, Bear, and Whale.

TUNDRA TURF

5 or 6 apples, peeled, cored, and sliced
2 tablespoons sugar
1 teaspoon cinnamon

½ cup each rolled oats, chopped pecans, flour, brown sugar, and butter

Preheat oven to 375°. Grease a 13- by 9-inch baking pan. Combine apples, sugar, and cinnamon in the greased pan; set aside. In a medium bowl, combine oats, pecans, flour, and brown sugar; cut in butter until mixture is crumbly. Sprinkle oat mixture over apples and bake for 25 to 30 minutes. Serves 8.

Streams and bogs dot the horizon, surrounded by flowers, berries, and lichen.

WILDERNESS TRAIL MIX

3 cups rice cereal squares
2 cups crisp chow mein noodles
¼ cup butter
1 teaspoon garlic powder
3 tablespoons teriyaki sauce
1 tablespoon sesame oil

Preheat oven to 250º. Lightly grease a foil-lined cookie sheet. In a large bowl, combine cereal squares and chow mein noodles; set aside. In a small saucepan, melt butter. Remove from heat and add remaining ingredients, whisking until blended. Drizzle sauce over cereal mixture, stirring until evenly coated. Spread mixture onto cookie sheet. Bake for 45 minutes, stirring every 15 minutes. Makes 6 cups.

Millions of wild animals roam across their vast Alaskan home.

WOLVERINES

¾ cup powdered sugar
¼ teaspoon salt
¾ cup peanut butter
2 teaspoons vanilla
1 cup chocolate chips, melted

In a medium bowl, combine powdered sugar and salt; stir in peanut butter. Add vanilla, stirring until blended. Shape into teaspoon-size balls and dip into chocolate. Refrigerate 20 minutes to harden. Makes 2 dozen.

Savage and fierce, testy and cross,
the stinky wolverine will show you who's boss!